BLACKTHORN

To Paul and Maggie -
with love + best wishes,
Cillian
July 1995

Gillian Allnutt was born in 1949 in London but spent half of her childhood in Newcastle upon Tyne. In 1988 she returned to live in the North East. Before that, she read Philosophy and English at Cambridge and then spent the next 17 years living mostly in London, working mostly as a part time teacher in further and adult education but also as a performer, publisher, journalist and freelance editor. From 1983 to 1988 she was Poetry Editor at *City Limits* Magazine. She has published three collections of poetry, *Spitting the Pips Out* (Sheba, 1981), *Beginning the Avocado* (Virago, 1987) and *Blackthorn* (Bloodaxe Books, 1994) She co-edited *The New British Poetry* (Paladin, 1988) and is the author of *Berthing: A Poetry Workbook* (National Extension College/Virago, 1991). She currently teaches creative writing and literature in adult education and works as a writer in schools.

GILLIAN ALLNUTT

Blackthorn

BLOODAXE BOOKS

ISBN: 1 85224 270 1

First published 1994 by
Bloodaxe Books Ltd,
P.O. Box 1SN,
Newcastle upon Tyne NE99 1SN.

Bloodaxe Books Ltd acknowledges
the financial assistance of Northern Arts.

Cover printing by J. Thomson Colour Printers Ltd, Glasgow.

Printed in Great Britain by
Bell & Bain Limited, Glasgow, Scotland.

For Kate, my mother and my niece

Acknowledgements

Acknowledgements are due to the editors of the following publications in which some of these poems first appeared: *All Lombard Street to a China Orange* (The West Press, Newcastle, 1993), *Aquarius, Beneath the Wide Wide Heaven* (Virago, 1991), *Blue Nose Anthology* (Blue Nose Press, 1993), *The Echo Room, Frankenstein's Daughter* (Stride, 1993), *High on the Walls: A Morden Tower Anthology* (Morden Tower/Bloodaxe Books, 1990), *The Jacaranda Review, The Page (Northern Echo), People to People, Poetry with an Edge* (Bloodaxe Books, new edition, 1993), *Singing Down the Bones* (The Women's Press, 1989), *Sixty Women Poets* (Bloodaxe Books, 1993), *Transformation: The Poetry of Spiritual Consciousness* (Rivelin-Grapheme Press, 1988) and *WEA (Northern District) Annual Report, 1992-93*.

'Nailish' is included on the cassette accompanying the series of workbooks, *Reading Women Writers*, published by the NEC/Virago (1991). 'About Benwell' was broadcast by Tyne Tees Television in a programme in the series *In a City Art* (Merlin Films, 1993).

I'd like to thank Northern Arts for a writer's bursary awarded to me in 1992. And I'd like to thank Elizabeth Victor, who shared with me her own love of literature, helped me open new doors into the dark of writing, and acted as my unofficial editor before I sent this collection out into the world.

Contents

I.

Bringing the Geranium in for the Winter

Almost dark, the rain begins
again. I steal into my own
October garden

with a small black bucketful of
compost and a trowel.
I kneel

as if you, beautiful
before time with your small pale flowers still
opening, were my soul

and God,
in spite of groundfrost
and the book of rules for growing,

could
exist, incomprehensible, companion of
the overcoming darkness in the grass and apple garden.

I return among the small grave stones
I made your borders with
to kneel, to feel

about, to, probing, put my trowel in, pull you from
your unmade bed,
your mad

dishevelled garden: lifted out of,
orphaned bit of
truth

your petals wet with
rain. It's rain I somehow am
no longer stiff with

now my hands
the barest hands I have
are briefly of this earth and have begun

to learn the part of
root and leaf
to live

with
potting and repotting.
So I set

you, lastly, in the dry
companionable kitchen
on a plate,

my table
laid with cloth of quiet
October light.

heart note

because we for a while had been living there my heart

thought it was a house with cupboards and an open fire
and a door giving onto
an impossible steep twisted stair my heart

thought it could have small uncurtained windows it could go on
being there under its tiles for the swallows
every year

love was already living in the house my heart

thought when we got there it thought it was
a letterbox a back door opening to
a garden it could walk in

it was nothing we had put there but before us it was

apple willow and a wilderness of
rose thorn thick and dark
and light with its daylong delicate flowers my heart

thought it had roots it thought it could cover its roots
with straw it thought it could carry on
lighting its every morning fire

because we as love for a while had been living there

New Year 1987

Brancaster   last bare light of the afternoon   the two of
us   that lonely ark   the sun
going down

beyond Hunstanton   where the sea   the growing dark of
us   was breaking and   I knew not how   would break
me to the bone

and long before the Romans   we walked on   the dip and shallow of
the afternoon abandoned
towards

Holkham   and before that bay   the sandbank and the half black
hulk of the wrecked ship   hope   that iron heart   how
I'd hanker after it

Fantasia

Love's not a sewing house. Love is a horse.
Love is the wind's horse whistling over the silver sand. We're sea legs.
Listen, the tide's gone out of us. We're spinsters. Listen,
the wind is tearing the tiles from the roof of our house.
The sun's lifeboat is lost, it's sailing away from us, leaving
our shadows behind us, long dead skins on the sand.

Imagine. Our shadows are spindles. Now we are
spinning the linsey-woolsey light into a long thread. Look,
it's already a quick silver saddle with reins as red as the sun's.
It's coarse and it's fine. It's embroidered
with distant coastlines. Love is a sea horse.

Love

Loneliness, learning to do up her laces early, little knows
that love is, even now, about
to kill her.

Love plucks chickens.
Love plaits with skill its black rope of hair.
Like a Chinese grandmother. Look.

Love is a bound foot. How can it learn to walk
in a landscape without hope
like the Gobi Desert?

Love is arthritic and looks as if it would like
to strangle her. Love says:
'I would like to strangle you.

It is only a joke.'
Loneliness does up her shoes with a neat double knot.
Love is a wishbone, stuck, in her throat.

Like willow

As if I stood still by the path at the edge of the wood
and let hope hollow my heart's truth
out of me – you go.

My roots hurt. They are groping.

Was it your word, or mine, that, like the wind, commanded?

Perhaps it was love, that lonely god, willed the earth away.

For all I know, love took you tenderly. I live
in my own quiet country, touching the water,
letting it grieve me.

The Unmaking

Old is this earthen room; it eats at my heart.
ANON

What if, in mourning, I – ?

The mountain knows me as I am unknowing
stone of its stone.

My capable uncomprehending hands.

And if sack cloth astounds me?

I could not imagine that
queer quiet queen, my heart, her earthen room.

What if, without understanding – ?

My mind, its glass bead game, its quick bright imitation
stone

and I, for its glistering –

What if the mountain, my unmaking, is?

Blackthorn

I like to imagine
the stars are something other than sewing-machines.

I am rooted, remote.

I guard the white embroidered whirlpools
of the wind.

Beyond the muted talk of angels there are quick black holes
like poems. In my heart

I hear the creak and shuttle of the earth's old bones,
the toil and spin.

I am the wake, the needle and the well
of wondering.

II.

North

Who can refuse to live (her) own life?
ANNA AKHMATOVA

I have a new river now.

Not yours, Anna, but nearer
your Neva, nearer.

New streets, now, Newcastle
still without trees.

It has hills and wind.

Shall I find my feet that love me? Shall I
refuse them?

See, I have come without shoes.

The hills talk lightly here of built ships. Little is left
me now, a bit of walking.

About Benwell

Perhaps there will always be yellow buses
passing and Presto's
and people with faces like broken promises

and shops full of stotties and butties and buckets and bubble bath
and bones for broth
where the poor may inherit the earth

and women who will
wade into the wind and waste with hope eternal
and kids like saplings planted by the Council

and William Armstrong's endless line
of bairns, whose names, in sandstone,
rehabilitate their streets of rag and bone

where bits of paper, bottle tops and Pepsi cans blow up and down
despondently, like souls on their own.
Perhaps there will always be unremembered men

and maps of Old Dunston and Metroland and the rough blown rain
and the riding down of the sun
towards Blaydon.

Home Start
for my damp 2CV6

Look at the long dark
hill down which the daft yellow bus with its top deck

full of people requested not to smoke
and comfortable with smoke

is not coming, not coming. Only the wind
and rain travel over the half-lit land

of a city
braving its own bare-legged history.

Is this what I chose?
The bus, when it comes, will be like a beautiful yellow rose

and tomorrow the sun will shine
for ever on

the sorry, boneless dogs
of Benwell – and my spark-plugs.

After The Blaydon Races

Look how the big yellow bus of the sun bowls breakneck into
        Benwell also.

Shall it not, for a while, be still, with its wheel flown off?

Shall the old yellow bus, October, stop and beautifully steep us
in its pennyworth of ale, its picnic

cloth of gold unfolded on the rough grass?

Look how it briskly bowls by the rough sky-grass where houses were
and the forgotten, poor, affectionate people are,

berates us not as does the law in its bald helicopter

but, like that ribald bus on its breakneck way to Blaydon,
braves us, hedging bets

before our houses, waving, wild at heart and unrepentant
as the river, with its staithes and bridges.

Spring, Newcastle

The hills can come into my house now.
I'll wake well. I'll work

at an open window. Buses roll by me.
Big yellow whales, like love.

What does it mean, provincial?
Must it be careful?

I'll comfort my soul, make curtains. I'll not
open my mouth.

An old blue bicycle waits for me
in the hall.

I've paper, pencil. What lets me live
in my house shall be

bright, empty, uphill.
Like truth.

Portrait of a Poet in the Kitchen

Anna Akhmatova, home of my barely constituted home, may I,

out of my sleepless nights, make yours, adoptive godmother,
all that I have and have not been and my hands making
salt pea soup, a poem.

May I commend to you all my already imagined murders
and my table.

Like her, you are here in your eyes. A thousand and one
mirrors remember now and the way the Neva flows
austerely.

Scoured is the soul's belonging.

By the uncurtained window may I remind you of, in their making
now, my spared, unsparing hills.

Clara Street

Many small stones are the sea's washboard.

Light on the step.

In the bare room, sleep.

On the windy street Polly makes her complaint.
I'll miss her

and the hills. I went to them on my bicycle
but they have no thoughts.

Love cannot be called. It comes
into leaf like the clematis by the yellow wall.

The river's a common language

and the lit stones of the yard
attentive.

Polly talks of little but.
Life is hard.

Many are the unprepared cathedrals of my heart.

Backyard

Soul in the warm bean light
of the afternoon

be, without wings, a hanging-basket
or a water-butt

and pot-whole to the wild seed-hoard
that waits.

For the porcelain moon is broken into
shards,

the heart's
small skull-plates

open.

Knock

If love took a lick at my red lion door
I'd lope off with it

to the lyke-wake of the hills,
my learnéd animals.

If love, like a wingbone, lay within me
I'd be quiet.

I'd bear with it,
the shoulderblade of bird or angel

broken in me,
anchoring.

Lord of my own heart's opening, guarded, lonely
lord, lend me

the lion and the ladybird light
of your being,

that I, in my loping and aching, might
look to it.

At the writing table

Her letter lies among those I have not yet been able to read.
She will write to me of Leningrad.

My shoulders would like to hide.

But the lamp with its blue shade loves me.
It is so irreparably still around it...

My shoulders would like not to be so broad

and the table not bare
of all but the razor-shell the North Sea laid at my door

last year. It is empty, half-open and whole.

My shoulders, irreparably
my own.

Shall I be able, still?

Letter to

Lend me four pieces of yellow paper for my delight.

Beautiful are your feet with shoes and they shall enrol
themselves in my most intimate thought.

Of the metaphysical waters of Tyne and of the hills
I shall think,

of my elliptical heart, of the moonlight
speaking with tongues.

Let me have pale yellow paper.

Let the soles of your feet leap up from it quickly.

Let there be something of bird and Bible
about your feet

and of their unbelonging. What shall I write?

There are the hills. There are black holes. There are a hundred
miles of solitude.

The waters of Tyne shall listen
to the moon-tongue

in my heart also. Let Solomon speak of festivals
of yellow paper

and of your feet, without shoes, for my delight.

Sunart

I remember the little disturbances of stone
our feet made there –

the call of the oyster-catchers
further along the shore –

the occasional car.
And if we were

careful, among the loch's accumulation of blue hills,
neither to close the soul completely

nor to break, by opening, that frail ligament
between the two halves of the ark

of any shell –
what were we listening for

as we held, still, the tiny wendletrap of April
in our cold wet hands?

A difficult hour. I remember the light
rain came out of nowhere, silently

the salt on my lips
was there.

Lighthouse, Ardnamurchan, Argyll

Bearable is the black ash bud.
Bearable, too, the bleak upland, the beautiful
abortive thorn.

But here, the word's made stone.

The earth comes to itself and is and always
shall have been.

Here, almost unendurably, I am.

In this belonging's nothing but
the wind, the wild
Atlantic.

Salt rain blinds the skin.

What's Elsinore – ?

The unimaginable log-book of the lighthouse keeper
gone.

A stubborn low house still stands,
the old sheep-pens, lashed
walls of stone.

III.

The Swastika Spoon

Because from the bathroom window he saw the Crystal Palace burn.

Because the war did happen.

My father came home from the burning of Belsen

with bits of it under his skin and the bowl of his heart in his hands

that would never be the same again, not ever his own again.

Because of that burning down.

And, in his pocket, proudly, the souvenir spoon.

Of light tin, slowly the bowl of it has worn down.

Barely is it a spoon.

The best of my life has been stirring the Bisto in.

And was Jerusalem.

Because.

Of my father in me there has been no burning down.

In 1945

My father sat down where Belsen had been
and no birds came.

He could not listen any more.

Later the roots and stars would bring him a daughter.

They'd try to hurt him through her
singing.

He'd make her a home, he'd tell her
'Old Macdonald had a farm'

but he'd never hear again.

His ears were clogged wells. Hart's tongue
covered them.

His legs lay dying of typhus and rags.

His heart was a burnt-out chapel.

All the old hymns dried up in him like lentils.

His shoulders bore with him. Because of the farm
before the war

he'd spare his Uncle Tom.

My father sat down where butter and eggs had been
laid out.

It was in a Dutch kitchen.

The stars shone down like bits of shrapnel.

Scrub as he would, his hands would not
come clean.

Bone Note

The makar's wierd is to be a wanderer.
'WIDSITH'

For you and the sea I would have stayed in Brighton.
Twenty years on

what you knew then wakes up in me.
I remember the story:

a boy growing up in a small Welsh working class town
picked up the violin

to play for the earliest silent films
for bread, jam.

At forty or so, in London then, you found the courage to unlearn
the old tune,

all you'd ever known,
to discipline your bones for Bach or Beethoven.

Heifetz you gave me, who, all on his own
played Bach, abruptly: sonatas, partitas for one violin.

I have nothing to play the records on.
I know them now. They are my own

uncelebrated solitude.
'This is a pleasure the man in the street knows nothing about,'
        you said,

and still you were not an elite.
You had learned to be quiet. You knew that

the soul has to find its own weird
way in the world. That old violin I laid

aside, when I left home.
Yet it can ache, it is my left arm's

loneliness, my fingers don't forget, my ear knows when the note
is out

and, as I learn to make my own tune
awkwardly, for discipline

I thank you and for solitude,
for what is hard,

for what, beyond the word,
begins in me and is bone-heard.

Saturnian

How much they matter, your stars, Mandelstam,
in the bare room where I write
behind hundred year old windows
all night.

What a god of lead the soul can be
in its silver lining.
Only the one word in the one constellation of words
will do for its shining.

Thomas Eckland

Tom to my sister and those few others who know me well. Used
    to living
deep inland, among small hills.
My sister keeps house.
We're cold and close. Sometimes I think the sea must sound
like the wind in the trees in the field
when it breaks loose.
No, I've no wife.
Master, they call me, because in my way I'm learned enough.
A dour and decorative word is God,
a spiralling road.
Myself. Stone-cutter. Occasional headstone.
Dry stone walls by trade.

Jehax

Mostly they were afraid of me.

I was tall and dark. Blue-black. I admired the moon
in my skin.

And mostly I was a king, though I was not
the son of a king. The old king
had no son.

Some trials were held to find who should succeed him.

I was fourteen when I climbed up on the Royal Stone
for the first time, felt it
foot me.

I'd outdone the others with my sling,
the small blue stone
I flung.

When I was a man, I thought my soul lived in that stone.

Now I know.

The stone lived with me
in a little bag of lion-skin,
afterwards

was hidden in the heart-roots of the unimaginable forest.

It was not passed on.

They thought my power was great.
And when I was a young man, so did I,
but I grew out of it.

Always my heart knew better.

My heart was a small wise animal within me.

To the Royal Stone they would come from world without end
to probe the sand,
mostly asking

me to make the rain –

for we were dying and our ancestors were dying too.
My heart would cry within me
for it knew.

Rain was the name of one of our gods. It came when it would.

Still I presided at the rituals
where smaller lighter men broke sacred vessels
in the sand.

We thought the unimaginable trees could ask for us as well.

And sometimes rain would come. But then

my long-deserted people let not go their thought
that I alone –

or that perhaps the sling-stone –

that within –

Maybe we thought –

Sometimes I think it did work like that.

Oboth

Utha was my wife. She howled as I left her.
She flung herself to the floor of the hut.
Packed earth it was and ashes.
I saw two little ridges of earth where she'd
dug her wooden boots in. Writhed and howled, she did.
No one was there, though they are with her now.
They are combing her hair down her back.

I am sad I had to leave my boots behind.
They'd cut them from me months before I left
because I could no longer walk but lay on the shelf
of the bed cut into the white wall by the stove.
I would not let my split boots out of my sight.
They sat side by side on the stool
and Utha did not sit on it.

I did not know my feet. I think they were white
but I felt nothing. And they did not know themselves.
Utha wrapped them in brown cloth.
She said it was an old chemise.
What is chemise? Chemise came with her
from the small town where she'd been a girl.
Chemise was before I knew her.

Forest was what we knew together. What was ours.
Edge of forest. That at our backs and before us
taiga, scrub, the coarse yellow flowers.
Carts coming over the rutted plain.
Carts that stumbled, stayed one night
then left at dawn loaded with logs of pine.
That was in summer. The short light months.

In winter, snow. Moon light of snow my boots loved.
How they let themselves in for it and were glad.
They shaped themselves to snow and me,
the hard ground that they knew.
Irith had to split them from me
with his heart-axe. Little axe
he had, tucked in his belt.

We'd sawn together and our lives were long.
It is quite hard to explain how, with each pine,
we'd come to it and known.
The first and last and inner ring.
How Irith, axe in hand, had quickly cut the tree
and how, because he was a kind man,
Irith came to cut my boots from me that day.

Arkit

There were times when I saw very little of Bordan. Times he'd walk
into the half-built boat-house of my dream
as if he were home.

I stayed on the headland, watching. When there was oak
I cut the hands of the hungering gods
into oar-blades.

He, being a long-wood man, headed the line inland.

It was ten days' walk away from the sea to the woods we knew
and ten days' walking back, two men to a tree,
across the plain.

Bordan held the horde of stars in his hand

that they might rest from their endless trekking.

As if they were lost axes, he loved them.

Nights when the new moon, caulked and comely, came
within sight of home, we drank to them
from our cups of oak-wine.

Lenten

Browses the bald head of the theologian, Beldever.
The boy plays in the dead leaves in the wood.
The oak bears up, with its leaves and buds, all winter.
Now the librarian nods.
Outside, they are cutting the tree for the cross.
By sundown it is roughly shapen.
Their curses have wakened the boy out of his dead wood,
who comes running with acorns.
The pen-handle Beldever holds in his thick and delicate hand
is made of horn.
There's hart's-tongue grown in the old well-hole in the yard.
The monks have lowered their tone.
The librarian passes, the dream of the rood in his head.
But for the blackthorn, this year, Beldever would have wed his Lord,
they've said. Down in the village
the boy has said it. Beldever – Old Bede – 's not dead.
And the crossed wood shall be borne –
from now, two Fridays – to the knoll
above the brown and budded orchard
where the boy lies buried.
And the monks shall walk with it
in the dark April day.

Preparing the Icon

Andrej Rublev (c.1370-c.1430) instructs his apprentices

Do not imagine, now, the austere sad face of John.
Before the snow falls, go to the forest.
Bring wood for the board. For days, while the stove remains
unlit in the studio, work that wood with chisel and plane
until it is smooth.
Break the ice on the water-butt then.
Prepare and apply to the board the first thin layer of gypsum
like a skin. Stretch the canvas. Then put on
a second layer of gypsum. When it is hard and dry, like bone,
rub it down till your shoulders are tired.
Draw the outline of John from the book of tracings,
the Authorised Version.
Begin your illumination with the background. Green.
Bring a bowl of eggs from the monastery farm.
Let him come loud and clear as a locust in your listening
to his God, ours. Break the eggs.
Use only the yolk for the dilution of your colours.
In the silence of falling snow and of the imagination's
cold dark halls, you'll know your own
austerity and John's.

At the Bellmaking

There was ice in the bowl
by the well

but with bread in his pocket
he went

out into the bone-blue dawn. Without
his father he went

through the thick unbearable
wood

till he came to the place where the dark had been
cleared

and where
all night in prayer

the monk had been making his big copper bell
with fire.

He thought he would wait while
he ate his bread

and when he was old, he told himself,
he would go.

*

The monk had nothing to do but blow
on his hands

for a while. The bell, in its great round
mould in the earth, was making. The child watched,

worried for him, as the man tried
not to forget

that mine of quiet
in the bone

he had made of listening
to God.

The monk tried not to imagine the big reverberations of
the bell

that would break like water over
the old stone

walls
of the monastery

but to listen now to the little bright tongues of
the earth that would tell

him the sun was about to break over
the hill

and to the silent tongue of the bell
in its making.

Mute, white must be
the heat

for the bell
to fire

whole and frail and beautiful as bone
or prayer.

*

The child watched the thin monk walking and thought
of the swan's bone

he had found that summer
when he was seven

and had thought fit
to be a soul-boat sailing along in the early morning. The sun

came over the hill.
The swan's

bone must be able to fly on its own,
must remember how

flying went, because it had been
part of a swan. The child had seen

the wild swan swinging over
the Russian plain.

The old jeweller speaks

My soul's hands were the strongest and most skilful
hands I had. At last my own

hands understood and ordered stones

from out the pits and bolt-holes of the earth. The dour

light hid, like loneliness, in them.

My own hands hobbled it. My soul's hands held

the fire and reservoir of it

until

the earth's heart beat
in every jewel

I made,

in every stone the word
was audible.

Fever Hospital, London, 1929

(for my mother)

Even the stars stop still in their indescribable spaces
to hear how it was to have scarlet fever
at five-and-a-half. They light up, listen, as you tell how,
alone, out of the universe, your mother came on a bus
and a train and a bus from Forest Hill to Tottenham
with a little case and how
in the little case there was always
a book, a couple of buns and a bit of knitting begun
for you. It was love, but you don't say so, because you're telling how
the too young nurses put you in black stockings, black boots
and a pale pink dress and sat
you on damp grass in the hospital garden and how,
because it was only April, you, at only five-and-a-half
got kidney trouble. Even the stars smile
as you tell of the specimens heated on Bunsen burners on a table
in the middle of the ward and tell how you taught yourself to read
because you were bored and how that was all
and how you yourself went back with your mother to Forest Hill.
How hopeful the stars are as they go off smoking because it is
all so incomprehensible.

My Cross

Great Aunt Agnes, with whose saintly name
Very little indeed will rhyme,
Gave me at my cavernous cold-water Christening
An appropriate gold cross but later on when no one was listening
Led me very secretly to understand that my cross was no ordinary
        Christian
Thing I must bear, but one pagan, strange and in fact Egyptian:
An ankh
For which I must thank
Her and the Lady with whom she travelled all about the earth
Being a Lady's maid in her narrow ship's berth.
I do thank her
For this rose-engravéd anchor
Which, when my soul-boat is all battered and adrift
On the unfathomable seas, finds a tiny cleft
Like the one in Rock-of-Ages-cleft-for-me
And fixes itself in there strongly
And makes an inviolable rocking home
Of my soul-boat until the seas are good and calm.
Ankh means life, says my Concise Oxford Dictionary
And I wonder why there is as yet no Insurance Company
With such a sturdy helpful name.
Perhaps I will start one. Great Aunt Agnes used to comb
My unholy difficult hair
Saying what-lovely-curls until I would have hit her
Except she always gave me a threepenny bit for my tin bank
With which I intend to start an Insurance Company called Ankh.

Cam

Always I'd one leg longer than the other.
I wrote seven letters to Camaria.
I sewed twelve handkerchiefs of fine blue linen for her.
'Lame' couldn't stop me leaping up at her.
I loved her in the cradle of the stars
and in the chair.
Camaria: 'the sea comes to'.
I could never not hear it at the night door.
The cow's bell coming slowly
from among the trees, the byre below
the small house on the hill's quiet side.
A lifetime's listening for.
The sour bread rising by the fire.
I'd walk before the dark
the day comes to.
My short leg strove.
I saw the little colours of lichen.
Sometimes I thought my longer leg would like
to walk further, alone.
I'd gather berries for the big blue bowl.
Some I washed for myself and some, carefully, for Camaria.

Morne

Morne was my name and the name of the mountain.

Cold moon, crossing the doorstone, came
in a dream of her then. I knew

my mother. Kettle and spoon could not.

Self a dark stone. I, seven. Took Morne
to the mountain. Set her down.

Tamora, the mountain

I left her there among the plantain and the stones.

The lizard came to inspect her with its tongue.

Cloud-shadows separated in their passing
over her. The stars stood

guardedly. The bare rock burned.

Tamora, tongue of stone.

Her telling, blown like sand, inherits nothing.

Only the bones of the girl I laid upon her
shall be quick with her

bare knowing.

Egrit

Egrit, old by then.
A leg I'd never loved was gone.
I walked with a stave of thorn,
proud of my understanding.

Tales were told in the hall.
I knew them as I knew the land,
its old light hills.
I did not listen when they talked of miracles.

As if the child could live and die again.
We'd set a stone.
I knew I'd not walk properly again
and I'd the vegetables.

Women without children, wild and thin
and clothed in brown.
Nothing about them
but walking. In my bones

I felt for them and further on,
where the old road makes an unexpected turn,
they sat down.
Slept.

One set her staff beside her
in the ground. It, while she slept, took root,
as if it woke, was
budded. They walked on. And then

we'd a tree of our own
and such and such a one already cured,
they said. An odd word,
miracle.

I looked to my own stave.
Thorn. I thought it would not,
when the wild March wind came on,
flower white again.

Nailish

My name meant crippled.

Stood, like God the Mother, on its sudden hill
our ordinary, extraordinary cathedral.

Swallows were like small dark angels
there, they said

and I could well imagine.
When from my narrow bed I heard the bells

my heart remembered that

the moon was like a small bent needle and my spine
was black.

But Julian would wash her hands of that and without haste
        or hark-back
would make well my walking

and my wasted leg,
my will. In that midsummer of my thought

the light was like skimmed milk.

Mary

They will say that I kept all these things in my heart
and pondered them.

They will write it down.
I'll forget

how I fought imagination. Was it my own
indisputable angel?

Shortly they'll say that God sent Gabriel. That's what
they'll write. And what

is Gabriel but the word for morning? Light
of the orange-blossom.

I'll remember the road to Bethlehem. How we said nothing.
I shall return

to be one who will gather the stars like volcanic stones
in her apron.

Mary to the Scribes

I am beyond you with my beautiful shoulders, who believed
you could name your God

with hammer and nail,
dumb me

with annunciation. I,

who could have hurled a hierarchy of angels
out of Heaven, have no home

in Nazareth or Bethlehem. I have
no name

by which, in any tongue, you may dismember me. I am

beyond you with my beautiful shoulders, who bore
with Gabriel, became

a ship of light and bone.

Conventual

For God in me had shoulders of warped wood
and was a well

made ill with holy water.

Like the bitter withy God in me was thin, a broken
spine, a broken

violin, a whole ship
burial

of sound. God was the excommunicated wind
and crooked as a thorn

or gargoyle. God had a withered hand, a tongue of wood
like half a castanet

and could no longer set a keel
of thought

upon the water at Monkwearmouth
as in Bede he could.

Camaria

I

The coral reefs are derelict cathedrals and the sea-grass
is no longer singing.

Of the fixed and wandering angels, who can tell? Each one's mislaid
itself. Each one's

a lost tongue or a lout.

Despair lies thick upon the waters, thick as dust
or sleep.

And of Camaria? Whose soul elaborates the sea's
caught up in it.

II

Dust does not dream of itself. Nor does it
doubt.

The beautiful reverberations of the bell are daunted.

This is the sleep of louts.

III

Camaria comes as sea-cow or the moon's clay
light.

She looks, from her rock, at the delicate water, ill
as the laughter of mislaid angels, quiet
as the bell.

Ereshkigal in the Rocking-Chair

I am resplendent here in the sacred rocking-chair of your heart.
I'll not put off the stained and tattered black I wore,
the rut and dirt, the roads I walked. Barefoot
I've broken stones for bread. And now I'll sit as cast
clout to the clean and upright rocking-chair you christened
Abraham. No more will I break the stem of Jesse
or my old clay pipe for him. I'll smoke tobacco
for the black madonna of my own delight. For I am
queen of the mystic, desolate night and of the solitary
moon. And you, on this mid-November afternoon
of mist and thought, would claim me as your own?
Then bring me the nuns, that demolition gang of wooden women.
Bring me the girl you were, the virgin Mary with her
sleeves on fire. Bring me your black and tattered
academic gown, your God, the literary men
and women you have loved and all
your little revolutions.

Notes

THE UNMAKING

The quotation is from 'The Wife's Complaint', a poem translated from the Anglo-Saxon by Michael Alexander in *The Earliest English Poems* (Penguin, 1966).

ABOUT BENWELL, AFTER THE BLAYDON RACES, CLARA STREET

Benwell is part of Newcastle's West End and scene of some of the riots in September 1991. Lord Armstrong, founder of the firm that eventually became Vickers Armstrong, built many of the houses for his workers in the 1890s and the streets are reputedly named after his children, though in fact he had none. Dunston is on the opposite, south bank of the Tyne, as are Metroland, a permanent funfair in the Metro Shopping Centre, and Blaydon, celebrated in the song *The Blaydon Races*.

AT THE WRITING TABLE

The quoted line is from Anna Akhmatova's poem 'Creation' in the sequence 'The Secrets of the Craft', translated by Richard McKane in *Selected Poems* (Bloodaxe Books, 1988).

THE SWASTIKA SPOON

When my father came home from the war, he brought with him a German spoon with a swastika stamped into the handle. Forty years later it is still in use in my parents' kitchen. His army regiment helped to liberate Belsen.

BONE NOTE

The quotation is translated from the Anglo-Saxon by Michael Alexander. See note to 'The Unmaking'. The poem is addressed to my violin teacher of 20 years ago, whose name I do not remember.

SATURNIAN

Mandelstam was born under the sign of Capricorn, as I was. Its ruling planet is Saturn.

THOMAS ECKLAND

Thomas Eckland is an imaginary man.

JEHAX, OBOTH, ARKIT, CAM, MORNE, EGRIT, NAILISH, MARY

These are souls who find themselves together in the Gathering-place-of-souls-between-incarnations. Each tells something of his or her most recent incarnation before forgetting it and going from the Gathering-place into another one. All except Mary are imaginary figures.

Jehax has been an ancient African king. *Oboth* has been a member of an imaginary tribe dwelling in the forests of Siberia. *Arkit* was a member of an imaginary pre-Anglo-Saxon community of boat-builders living on the coast of Northumberland. *Cam* lived on a farmstead by a Norwegian fjord in the nineteenth century. *Morne* died when she was seven. *Egrit* witnessed an incident in the story of Etheldreda (*c.* 630 – 679), which took place during Etheldreda's flight, with two nun companions, from Coldingham (near Berwick) to Ely. *Nailish* lived in Durham some time after the lifetime of Julian of Norwich (born 1342), author of *Revelations of Divine Love*. In her book Julian writes, unusually, of God the Mother.

PREPARING THE ICON, AT THE BELLMAKING

Very little is known about the Russian icon painter Andrej Rublev (*c.* 1370 – *c.*1430). The bell-casting is based on my vivid memory of the bell-casting scenes in Andrej Tarkovsky's film *Andrej Rublev*.

MY CROSS

With thanks/apologies to Stevie Smith for her poem 'My Hat'.

CONVENTUAL

As a child Bede lived in the monastery at Monkwearmouth before moving, at the age of 14, to the newly-founded monastery at Jarrow.

CAMARIA

Camaria is an imaginary goddess. I wrote the poem during the Gulf War in 1991 when Saddam Hussein turned the oil taps on in the sea.

ERESHKIGAL IN THE ROCKING-CHAIR

In ancient Sumerian myth Ereshkigal was Goddess of the Underworld.